SUCCESS & BEAUTY TALK

WOMAN EMPLOYEE TO WOMAN ENTREPRENEUR

CHARLOTTE HOWARD

WOMEN LIFE MENTOR + 44X'S INTERNATIONAL BEST SELLING PUBLISHER + AUTHOR

Charlotte Howard - Heart Centered Women Publishing

108 Flintlock Lane

Summerville, SC/USA 29483

www.heartcenteredwomenpublishing.com

charlotte@thehairartistassociation.org

Book Cover ©2015 Charlotte Howard - Heart Centered Women Publishing

Book Layout ©2015 Charlotte Howard - Heart Centered Women Publishing

Ordering Information:

Quantity sales. Special discounts are available on quantity purchases by corporations, associations, and others. For details, contact the "Special Sales Department" at the address above.

Success & Beauty Talk: Woman Employee to Woman Entrepreneur Charlotte Howard. —1st ed.

ISBN-13: 978-0692365748

ASIN: 0692365745

DEDICATION

This book is dedicated to all of the women who are employees and want to become a successful woman entrepreneur. That's YOU! Yes YOU!! It is my hope that this book empowers you to use your god given talents to build a real sustainable income doing what you love.

Wishing YOU love, peace and happiness!!

Charlotte Howard
Women Life Mentor, Award-Winning Hair Artist & 44X'S International Best Selling Author and Publisher

APPRECIATION

I'm grateful to god for all that he continues to do for me without him I do not know where I would be today. I'm grateful for my family and friends for being supportive and a very special thanks to my amazing kids Daija Howard, Daivontae Howard, Destiny Howard and Da'Kari Howard for being so understanding while mom continued to do all of her personal, business and life projects. I want to give special thanks to my mentors Marquetta Breslin, Fabienne, Fedrickson, Dr. Stacia Pierce, Lisa Marie Rosati, Ann Sieg, Pam Perry and Leonie Dawson for being such amazing mentors in my life + business.

Finally I want to thank YOU for purchasing Success & Beauty Talk: Woman Employee to Woman Entrepreneur. It is my mission to empower millions of women and because of women like YOU I'm closer to reaching my goal.

Live life, love fully and laugh often!

With Love,

Charlotte Howard
Women Life Mentor, Award-Winning Hair Artist & 44X'S International Best Selling Author and Publisher

CONTENTS

INTRODUCTION

Among the hardest transitions for women is to move from the employee to the entrepreneur mentality. The idea of getting on your own, getting your own business is incredible.

It's the desire of a lot of women to leave their jobs and get to be successful business owners.

However, is there a transition that has to be made from the employee mentality to the entrepreneur mentality?

It's really exceedingly crucial that you create an entrepreneur mentality to succeed in business on your own...because most of the principles you'll need to succeed are based off of being a true entrepreneur.

And there is a BIG difference between that and an employee mentality, I'm not pulling your leg ...and I will put it all on the table here to make sure you understand what I mean.

Live life, love fully and laugh often!

With Love,

Charlotte Howard ·
Women Life Mentor, Award-Winning Hair Artist & 44X'S International Best Selling Author and Publisher

1 CREATING A BEAUTIFUL FOUNDATION

Many small business women started their beginning as an employee. They worked for somebody else. However, if you've been an employee for years, it may be difficult to shake off the employee mentality.

What does this mean???

If you have an employee mentality, you're more likely to look to other people to tell you what to do. You'll find it difficult to take responsibility for the success and failure of your personal and professional endeavors.

As an employee, you have no say about how business is done. You just work hard to prove your value so you can stay employed.

Which One Are You???

If you're a woman entrepreneur, you think much differently. Essentially the buck stops (and begins) with you. You're responsible for the success and failure of your personal and professional endeavors. You are the one who makes all the huge decisions (including who to designate smaller decisions to!).

To discover if you're thinking like a woman employee or woman entrepreneur, take this fast quiz:

• Do you confine your tasks/responsibilities to a subset of what is required for your business to flourish?
• Do you base your life-style on your revenue?
• If a money setback happens, do you shrink your budget to adapt to the reduction in revenue?
• Do you constantly seek outside advice to make even daily decisions?

If you responded "yes" to most of these queries, chances are you have a woman employee mentality. Here's why those with a woman entrepreneur mentality would answer "no."

Do you confine your tasks/responsibilities to a subset of what is required for your business to flourish?

Women entrepreneurs understand that occasionally they have to do things in their business that are "higher up" or "beneath" their skill level. Their mental attitude is if it has to get accomplished, get it accomplished and they're not adverse to bundling up their sleeves and getting their arms dirty.

Do you base your life-style on your revenue?

Women entrepreneurs will seek to develop their business, enlarge their line of products and broaden their services when money setbacks happen. They don't let themselves get to be or remain a victim of fiscal conditions.

If a money setback happens, do you shrink your budget to accommodate the reduction in revenue?

Women entrepreneurs send out the payments for themselves first. They center on bringing in the money that supports the life-style they want and invest the rest into their business. With that being said, they accept the sacrifices that may need to be made in order to achieve a goal.

Do you constantly seek outside advice to make even daily decisions?

Women entrepreneurs handle their time and take responsibility for their actions. While they might seek out mentors to guide them to expanded growth, they're in control of their day-to-day actions and don't need somebody else to tell them what to accomplish or prompt them to accomplish it.

Let's look at some more differences

Monday mentality

• Women employees fear Monday. (Or, whatever the beginning day of their work week is.)

• Women entrepreneurs are not bolted into a work week. They approach each day as a different chance to go after their dreams.

It's not my problem mentality

• Women employees have this mentality they view everything on the job by whether or not it's their problem.

• Women entrepreneurs view everything as their duty as they have ownership of what is happening in their business.

T. G. I. F. (Thank Goodness It's Friday) mentality

• Women employees are constantly looking forward to their off days.

• Women entrepreneurs are forever seeking ways to extend their business even when they're not "working" they're considering ways to extend their entrepreneurial talents. They look forward to each day!

When am I going to receive a raise? mentality

• Women employees think that raises ought to come according to the calendar, instead of according to their work.

• Women entrepreneurs seldom consider when they'll receive an increase. They realize that the more they work towards helping other people the greater their reward will be.

Oh no, what now mentality

• Women employees set about meetings with an "oh no" mentality.

• Women entrepreneurs set about meetings with a mastermind mentality. They realize that excellent ideas come out of these meetings.

There are a lot more mindsets that we may compare. As a matter of fact if a few have come to mind for you as you read this write them down.

1. _____

2. _____

3. _____

4. _____

5. _____

2 PURSUING YOUR BEAUTIFUL DREAM

There are a lot of women employees who are longing to be their own boss, yet are fearsome of what the future may hold if they were women entrepreneurs. I would like to advise you that if you are among those women, you'd do well to become an extraordinary woman employee first! I spent over a decade as a woman employee and was constantly found to be a model woman employee.

My women entrepreneurial bosses constantly gave me high evaluations. In going over the list of women employee mentalities, I can frankly tell you that I didn't have those mentalities. I was an extraordinary woman employee!

If you have a want to be on your own one day, going after your dreams as a woman entrepreneur, you are able to begin now. Approach your occupation as though you owned the company where you work.

Bearing that ownership spirit will reward you on the job and prepare you for the day when you are able to pursue your own business. You are able to be a woman entrepreneur while you're still working. Having this spirit will excite you to go after your own personal and professional endeavors when you're not on your employer's time clock.

Positive Mindset and Productivity

You spend about a one-third of your life at work. If you're spending it with negative people, it may really affect you and bring you down.

By controlling negative thoughts as they enter your ears and not letting them go forward in your thoughts, you'll be doing a lot of the work to remain positive in a negative situation and build your business skills. Here are ways to keep horrible situations at work from bogging you down.

Possess a life outside your job.

Keep acquaintances who have a good grasp of reality and with whom you are able to share life that's totally unrelated to the job you do. Refuse to even discuss your work outside work hours, particularly if the environment is toxic except when it comes to the ideas for your own business.

Recognize that most of what goes on at work and most of the negativity, even when directed at you.

Think about the stress your colleagues are facing at work, at home and in their personal lives and comprehend that they're projecting and displacing their anger onto you and other people around them as well. Remember that dealing with people is crucial to being a woman entrepreneur.

Refuse to let your colleagues' workaholic, ambitions and selfish conduct seep into your system.

It's simple to start letting negative conduct creep in by agreeing with perspectives or taking sides. Rather, choose to rise above it all by staying neutral.

Defend your thoughts; they sooner or later become your reality.

Make certain the negativity around you doesn't continue playing in your head. Play music at your desk at a reasonable volume if you think it helps center you. Take breaks to collect your thoughts. Keep favorable reminders in quotes and pictures around your work space about what you are trying to learn and accomplish.

Truly think about your options for beginning your entrepreneurial journey.

A few bosses may be emotionally abusive; if the company surroundings don't look likely to change, evaluate whether this is truly the best place for you and ways you can start your own thing soon.

You spend eight plus hours a day at your desk juggling calls, e-mails and correspondences. All the same the stack of paper on your cluttered up desk continues growing taller, you eat more meals at the office than you do at home and you're still hardly meeting your deadlines.

Discover ways to keep away from time traps and to improve existing procedures to be not only more productive at work, but much less stressed and to develop skills that you can use in your own business.

Notice time wasters.

Standard culprits are instant messaging, net surfing, personal calls and gossip with colleagues. The minutes spent on these distractions may become hours of lost time and lost productivity. Determine limits on these actions and discover ways to politely end conversations.

Confine distractions and interruptions.

Schedule times to follow-up and respond to mail, e-mail and voice mail. If conceivable, switch off instant messenger programs and don't answer personal calls while you work at other tasks.

Coordinate and prioritize.

If you're consistently searching for items on your cluttered up desk, allow time to organize files, tools and equipment. Keep paper and electronic files in marked folders. On your PC, produce shortcuts and favorites to help find items rapidly and easily.

Utilize a single portable calendar to track all meetings, dates and deadlines.

Produce a schedule to begin and finish a given task and stick to it. Start and finish tasks on time. A daily or weekly "To Do" list may likewise be a helpful tool to stay on track and remain productive.

Be truthful with yourself about your projects and deadlines and then budget time accordingly. It may be helpful to do the things that you like the least first, as they might be more time consuming and you're more likely to finish more interesting activities.

Compose agendas for meetings and remain inside the allotted time.

Inefficient meetings that go late are a huge cause of productivity loss. Put down all key information like date, time, attendees, schedule items and action items when taking notes. This might save considerable guessing later. When in doubt, document.

Learn to utilize new and better tools to accomplish your work and invest a little time in learning to utilize existing tools more efficiently.

Discover a coach or mentor or take a class in time management, organizational strategies and productive business communication.

Take breaks.

This might seem conflicting when you are swamped. All the same, "crunch time" is when it's even more crucial to stay clear and centered. It's easy to make errors and when feeling overworked.

Actually schedule breaks into your day if essential. Even a short walk around the building may clear your head and bring down stress, which promotes productivity.

3 FOCUS ON YOUR BEAUTIFUL CUSTOMERS

Watch and learn from everyone you work with because they frequently demonstrate the habits you'll need to have when you're living the life of a woman entrepreneur like how to listen to customers.

Notice What People Want

There's a lot of discussion about listening these days. Listening is among the most crucial skills that you are able to learn. If you are able to really stop and listen to your customers, you are able to pave the path to ongoing business success.

Listening calls for paying attention and reacting to the needs and wants of customers. If you want to have your own business, you have to practice the art of active listening.

It is not good enough to react to clients. You have to be able to anticipate their needs. Listening to clients is about placing your company at the forefront to be the answer to the buyer needs and a solution provider.

Listening is likewise about getting involved with your clients. This includes really spending time with them, exploring things that are significant to them, studying magazines and books that are written for them, and being an authority in the things that matter to them.

Your business should have an ideal customer. This is the prototype of the perfect client for you. You need to draw in this type of client, and the more of your clients that fit the ideal, the better. So, it adds up that this is the sort of client you should be paying close attention to.

A client is somebody who's purchased from you or your company you work for, but it's likewise somebody who may purchase from you. You should treat clients, prospects, and general public with equal respect.

You should also spend your time listening to people who you most want as clients.

Listening should occur everyplace. That being said, you are able to hone your listening skills by utilizing specialized tools and strategies.

Offline, you should be conducting client surveys and just be getting out and talking to clients and people. Go to trade shows and conferences that are likewise attended by your ideal clients. If there are none in your area, begin one.

As your expertise grows, you might want to think about doing a few speaking engagements. This is an awesome way to meet people and get them to tell you about the problems that they are facing.

Online, the openings are endless. You are able to listen on Twitter with the help of Twitter Search. You are able to track key words and phrases across the internet utilizing Google Alerts.

Forums are a great place to listen. You are able to likewise produce your own listening posts with a blog, radio show or podcast. Sure, this is about you talking, but it will likewise force you to explore and learn about your clients. And you are able to encourage dialog and reader comments.

Make sure to listen where clients are talking. You will be able to find out where ideal clients congregate, online and offline, you have to be there too.

Active listening will help you to better comprehend and connect with your clients. It will make sales and marketing easier, as you'll be able to position yourself right between the client and their needs.

Becoming a great listener will lead you to the people you wish to reach. Everybody loves being listened to. So close your mouth, put away that profit and loss sheet for a minute, and begin exploring the world of your clients.

4 BE A BEAUTIFUL PROVIDER

We all supply value in the workplace—either by the work we inject as a woman employee, or with the products and services we sell in our business.

A great performance review might not be enough to guarantee a promotion or even to keep your line of work. In addition to that, a high-quality product or service might not be enough on its own.

Give First Mentality

Value is in the eye of the observer (think about how much more you may pay for a place to stay on a showery day). Workers who are simple to get along with and reliable with assignments will be more useful to their manager than somebody who produces stress in team meetings and on a regular basis misses deadlines.

In addition to that, a product will be more useful to a consumer if her favorite famous person endorses it, if it's on sale, or if it includes a contributed bonus.

At the same time, we're becoming hypnotized to ads; we've gotten to be wary of bonus offers, upsells and add-ons. We're seeking authenticity; that's what we value today.

Given the expanded rivalry in the job market, workers have to establish their value to the company in order to get and keep their lines of work, as well as to move ahead to higher positions and acquire customers when it comes to having the woman entrepreneur mindset.

A lot of consumers are feeling whipped and worried and are guarding their purchases cautiously. On the other hand, we're in the middle of a virtual flood of sales offers (no deficit there).

Consumers are picking out the products and service they perceive to be the most useful. You absolutely have to maximize the sensed value of what you offer. But you likewise need to support yourself and your loved ones. So what do you do?

Seek things you are able to add on to your products and services that won't cost you a great deal but are still really useful, e.g., a downloadable e-book or accompanying CD.

Approach somebody who has a complimentary business that services your market, and ask her to chip in an additional product or service. It's a win-win, as they acquire the exposure to your clients or customers and you get the extra value for your offer.

Add to the sensed value of your product or service by including case studies and/or recommendations. Think about who may have the peak level of "societal capital" for your audience.

Typically this will be somebody whom your leads may relate to as having like challenges and conditions OR somebody they look up to for having accomplished what they're attempting to accomplish.

Once you consider ways to ramp up the sensed value of what you provide, put yourself in your customer's shoes. Is there something about your product or service that you brush aside, but that other people find useful? If you're not certain, survey satisfied buyers and customers.

Women employees and entrepreneurs, make yourself essential to your team by demonstrating yourself as a connector. Listen for matters that people require and match them with people, products or services that have them.

Naturally, do this for work projects and additional office tasks, but likewise extend it to personal issues.

For instance, if somebody tells you about an awesome holiday spot, and somebody else is planning their next trip, suggest that the two individuals chat about it.

Point out the added value you're already giving to your customers. Maybe you regularly catch clues that everybody else misses. Don't simply assume your clients will notice: point them out in an email or blog post.

In this crowded market, competitive business market and challenging economy, there are chances for the cream to rise to the top. Make certain you remind people of your value; why you're the cream as a woman entrepreneur.

5 FIND A BEAUTIFUL MENTOR WITH EXTRAORDINARY COACHING

A mentor is a person with more experience in business, or merely in life, who may help a woman entrepreneur hone her powers and advise her on piloting fresh challenges.

A mentor may empower women entrepreneurs in a broad array of scenarios, whether they supply pointers on business technique, bolster your networking crusades or act as confidantes when your work-life balance becomes out of whack. However the first thing you need to know when seeking out a mentor is what you're seeking from the arrangement.

What having a personal trainer is to your body, having a coach may be to your mind. Utilizing a coach appears to be the latest way for some individuals to get ahead in today's gaga business world.

Learn From Others

What may your mentor do for you? Ascertaining what type of resource you require is an imperative first step in the mentor hunt. Beginning with a list is a good opening. You might want somebody who's a great listener, somebody socially connected, somebody with expertise in, suppose, marketing, person accessible.

Ideally you may find a mentor with all of these characters, but the reality is you might have to make a few compromises. After you count the characters you're looking for in a mentor, split up that list into wants and needs.

The following step is to "do an informational interview with many candidates and then go back to your standards that way you don't get blown away by chemistry and you remain centered on your business or personal reasons for needing a mentor. By judging a combination of the qualitative and quantitative properties of each of your likely mentors, a prime candidate will come forth.

Bear in mind that it might be advantageous to have more than one mentor. If you think that you might monopolize too much of your mentor's time then several mentors might be the answer.

The benefits of having multiple mentors is that you are able to get a lot of assorted viewpoints and when you have many mentors at a time, if they're seated around a table, the synergy between the mentors truly helps move your thinking along.

How to discover a mentor:

Begin with loved ones and friends - When seeking a mentor, begin close to home. Really close to home. Occasionally you are able to talk to your own relatives or friends, individuals who you trust, who you know, who you are able to sit and say 'gee, what do you feel about this?

Think about those in your broadened network - If your friends and loved ones provide you enough unsought advice already, and you don't believe that's the route for you, your left over options are people who don't know you as well or don't know you in the least yet.

How do you ask for such a huge commitment from a virtual stranger? The opening move is to get hold of your network of contacts. A positive word from a common acquaintance may go a long way toward getting a mentoring relationship off to a great start.

Additionally, you shouldn't pick out a mentor overnight, which implies you ought to keep your antenna poised to pick up on likely mentors at conferences, trade shows, masterminds and so forth. Meeting with a future mentor in person helps construct a rapport and you may wish to wait till that connection develops before tossing out the question.

Think about total strangers - perhaps none of the individuals in your network seem like a great fit for you. Begin doing a little research. Profiles of business owners in magazines and papers may key you in to somebody who equals your style. But when you have a few prospects go forward delicately.

Discover as much as you are able to about the likely mentor and attempt to schedule a brief interview by telephone saying you have a few particular questions or simply generally wish to pick their brain.

You ought to travel to them and, particularly at first, make it as simple for them to help you as you are able to. At the end of your beginning interview, if it appears to have gone well, you may consider the idea of speaking once again, whether by Skype, telephone or in person, sometime in the time to come.

Over time, if they feel receptive, you may bring up the idea of a more conventional mentoring relationship with more particular parameters and goals.

Think about the rivalry - Well, not your direct rivalry. For instance, if you're in retail selling jewelry, somebody selling clothes isn't in direct rivalry with you but may still have a few insights into the fashion industry.

If you have a brick and mortar store, you may even call somebody who does precisely what you do in a far away location, suppose you're in New York City and they're in South Carolina.

However the web is increasingly placing retailers even on different continents in rivalry, so step lightly. A different hint would be to seek out counsel from somebody at a business larger than yours who may be less likely to view you as rivalry.

Tap your field - your suppliers, your local chamber of commerce, and relevant trade publishing are great sources for likely mentors. These are all great places to come by knowledgeable people, but how do you find somebody who matches your personal flair? Look for a mentor the same way that people look for hairstylists or medical professionals, seek recommendations.

Pay for mentoring - But what if you have an awesome idea that you wish to get off the ground rapidly, and you need a fast jolt of expertise? Great informal mentorships are cultivated bit by bit and may frequently last for years. If what you require is a crash program, it may be time to bring in the consultants.

Individuals at all stages of professional evolution need coaches to help them. Women CEO's often utilize coaches to bounce ideas around, women entrepreneurs utilize their coach to help them think strategically about the business, and coaches help other people sort out career decisions.

Think about the affect you are able to have by offering to coach your partners, employees and customers. You are able to be a coach to the people around you and help them to accomplish their goals faster and simpler.

Individuals seek coaches for 2 basic causes:

• A few people look for coaches to help them discover a balance between their personal and professional lives.

• Other people want coaches to help them get more productive in their business or help step-up their business.

People aren't looking for speedy answers any longer. They're seeking ways to produce lasting change. The traditional consultant doesn't truly bring about lasting change. A coach is a sort of consultant who works with customers to come up with their own changes that are lasting.

Coaching is the next evolutionary stage of consulting. Coaching is a blend of business, finance, psychology, philosophy, transformation and spirituality. It helps individuals get more of what they wish out of life, whether it's business success, fiscal independence, academic excellence, personal success, physical wellness, relationships or career planning.

Coaches are soundboards, support systems, cheerleaders and teammates all rolled into one. Bottom line; the job of a coach is helping other people realize their total potential.

Coaches utilize questioning skills, listening and motivational strategies to help individuals build the skills, knowledge and confidence required to better their professional and personal lives.

A coach is a collaborative partner who helps you achieve things. Coaching isn't a replacement for personal responsibility and personal alteration or choice.

You require a coach if:

• Your business isn't performing as well as you wish.
• You feel you're working harder and are less gratified.
• Your business is doing well and you're getting sick of working so hard.
• A big downsizing in your company is causing big change in the work surroundings.
• You think your career is approaching a plateau.
• You got a sub par performance review.
• You're not able to mold and lead your staff.
• You're not easy making strategic conclusions.

A coach supplies you with a place to get a little perspective. A coach is somebody who isn't caught up in all the daily stuff and who may see the big picture.

Once I decided to follow up on my entrepreneurial journey the conversion from woman employee to woman entrepreneur was easier because I initially developed the entrepreneurial spirit while working and utilized the time to keep an eye on situations and formulate the skills I would need in order to be successful.

You are able to transition to an entrepreneur mentality too and I trust you will.

ABOUT THE AUTHOR

Charlotte Howard is a Women Life Mentor to women wanting to create fulfillment + happiness in their lives. She has a unique ability in getting women to take immediate action on creating fulfillment and happiness using a heart-centered systematic approach which empowers women to produce impeccable results, in record time.

She is an accomplished Award-Winning Hair Artist + Success + Beauty Talk Radio Show Host + Best Selling Book Expert who published over 40 International Best Selling Book Titles. She is all about women empowering women to create a renewed sense of energy and motivation for enhancing themselves, lives and business from the inside out!

Born in Charleston, South Carolina, United States Ms. Howard had been diagnosed with carpal tunnel syndrome, mentally + physically abused as a young woman, but she became empowered by getting mentorship from other women in her life that encouraged her to become a better woman.

With the self confidence and self-esteem of a determined single mom + heart centered woman, Ms. Howard now uses her god given talents to teach women how to look + feel beautiful from the inside out.

Ms. Howard's International Best Selling Book Series Success In Beauty has been co-created with heart centered women all over the world to continue her mission of empowering millions of women of all ages to be more inspired, more confident and ready to take immediate action on pursuing and achieving their ideal goals, passions and dreams.

"She believes that each of us has a personal calling that's as unique as a fingerprint – and that the best way to succeed is to discover what you love and then find a way to offer it to others to make their lives better."

Learn more about Ms. Howard by visiting www.SuccessInBeauty.net and www.CharlotteHowardInfo.com

She can empower YOU to:
- Create a Beautiful, Sexy and Confident New You
- Create a Confident, Successful New Beauty Salon Business
- Create a Confident, Successful New Business
- Create a Meaningful Book
- Create a Meaningful Anthology
- Create a Meaningful Talk Radio Show

Charlotte can be reached at:

Phone: (803) 414-2117 Skype: CharlotteEmryHoward

About Me | Brand Yourself | Hair Artist Association | Twitter |
Facebook | Linkedin | Pinterest

Visit www.BeautySalonSuccessCoach.com to watch FREE webinar that shows how Charlotte transitioned from woman employee to woman entrepreneur. She can empower YOU too!!

www.ingramcontent.com/pod-product-compliance
Lightning Source LLC
Chambersburg PA
CBHW070723210326
41520CB00016B/4435